8.93   R. Stewart

A POCKET BOOK
OF
HEALING

By
DAVID A. MACLENNAN

ONE CRANBOURNE ROAD, LONDON N10 2BT

©—*Arthur James Limited*, 1963

First English and Commonwealth Edition published
1963

First Paperback Edition 1979

No. 2 Devotional Pocket Book Series

The American copyright of this devotional Pocket Book of Healing is held by The Upper Room.

Copyright strictly reserved.

ISBN 0 85305 220 4

MADE AND PRINTED IN GREAT BRITAIN BY
PURNELL AND SONS, LTD. PAULTON (SOMERSET) AND LONDON

CONTENTS

CHAPTERS	PAGE
I. GOD WANTS YOU TO BE WELL	11
God's Plan May Be Blocked	13
God Gave Us Christ	15
Disease Is the Enemy Christ Fights to Overcome	16
Scripture to Strengthen	19
Assurances and Prayers	19
II. ALL HEALING IS DIVINE	23
Through Many Ways	25
Which Is the Best Way for God to Heal?	26
Doctors Are Divine Healers	28
Prayers	31
For Doctors and Nurses	31
For All Engaged in Healing	32
For Research Workers	33
A Psalm for the Hospital	34
A Blessing	35
III. THE GREAT PHYSICIAN NOW IS NEAR	36
By the Name of Jesus	37
How Christ Comes to Us	39
The Risen Lord Welcomed	42

CHAPTERS	PAGE
Prayers for His Presence	43
Trust and Confidence	43
For Times of Pain	44
We Commend unto Thee	45
IV. WHEN GOD SEEMS TO SAY "NO"	47
Sincere Prayers Answered	48
God Always Heals	56
Prayer for God's Presence	60
Prayer for the Dying	61
V. WHEN IT HURTS TERRIBLY	63
Bring It to Him	65
Ask God to Use It	66
Christ Is Master of Pain	68
Prayers	70
We Offer Our Gift of Pain	70
The Peace of Pain	72
A Prayer to Accept Pain	74
VI. DEEP PEACE HELPS GOD HEAL US	76
How Do We Experience God's Peace?	77
Christian Affirmations	82
Then What Are We Afraid Of?	83
Ask and Receive	84
God Is Your Guardian	85

CHAPTERS	PAGE
Christ's Cure for Worry	86
Live One Day at a Time	87
Suggestions for Prayer in Time of Illness	88
When You Are Sick	88
When Another Is Sick	89
A Prayer Concerning Hope	91
A Prayer to Recover Hope	92
For Christ's Blessing	93
Before an Operation	94
VII. THE HEALING COMMUNITY	96
The Church—Christ at Work	96
Releasing Healing Power	97
Prayers	103
A Blessing	105
Thanksgiving for Recovery	105
AUTHORS' INDEX	107
ACKNOWLEDGMENTS	109

FOREWORD

"*Jesus Christ heals you*" (Acts 9: 34). Peter's assertion expresses the faith of the Church, and the conviction of this little book's author.

Christians should believe that God's perfect will for every one of His children is health in the deepest and most comprehensive meaning of the word. God gave Himself to us in Jesus Christ that we might have abundant life, here and hereafter. God uses many instruments and agents to achieve His purpose: physicians; surgeons; nurses; our faith and prayers; the Church, which is the body Christ uses in the world today; and the mysterious and direct action of the living Christ, or Holy Spirit.

A famous British surgeon, Lord Moynihan, was invited to operate before a group of distinguished doctors. Afterwards, one of them expressed his admiration and surprise that the surgeon could do his work so calmly and well, undisturbed by onlookers. "When I operate," he said, "there are just three people in the theatre—the patient and myself." "But that is only two," said the other. "Who is the third?" "God," was the reply. God is present in every operating theatre, in every hospital room and ward, in every home, in every person, seeking to give His children newness of life.

May the pages which follow help to create conditions in which Christ's healing love may be most fully experienced. "Doctor" Luke, in his Gospel, tells us that when ten persons suffering from a dreaded disease called on Jesus to help them, Jesus immediately responded. This is what happened when they responded to Jesus' request, *"And as they went they were cured"* (Luke 17: 14. Goodspeed). As you go through these pages into the presence of the living Christ, may the same wonderful blessing be yours.

DAVID A. MACLENNAN

I

GOD WANTS YOU TO BE WELL

God wants you to be well. This is the truth taught by the Bible, demonstrated by God's beloved Son our Lord Jesus Christ, and confirmed by the Holy Spirit in the experience of the Church across the centuries. To be completely well means to be truly whole. Wholeness includes the health of the total person—body, mind, and spirit. Health in this comprehensive sense is what the Bible means by salvation. In both the Old Testament and the New, the word translated "salvation" means "bodily health" as well as "general safety and security." It is so used in Matthew 9:21 and Luke 8:36. The woman who had suffered for twelve years came up to Jesus to touch the fringe of His garment, "*For she said to herself, 'If I only touch his garment, I shall be made well.'*" Jesus, the divine Physician, sensitive to her need and to her touch gave her the assurance she sought: "*Take heart, daughter; your faith has made you well.*"

Our Scriptures clearly show that God's purpose for all His children is that they should be saved. To be saved is also to enter into newness of life mentally, physically, emotionally. According to the New Testament, salvation means becoming nothing less than a new creation. J. B. Phillips translates Paul's words of 2 Corinthians 5: 17–18: "*For if a man is in Christ he becomes a new person altogether—the past is finished and gone, everything has become fresh and new. All this is God's doing, for he has reconciled us to himself. . . .*"[1]

[1] See pages 109 and 110 for this and similar references.

GOD'S PLAN MAY BE BLOCKED

Why then is there sickness in the world God made and loves? No human being knows the whole answer to this hard question. One reason for sickness is that God gave us the precious gift of freedom to choose to live by the laws of health, the laws of the Kingdom of God, or to reject these laws. He knew this freedom is needed for us to grow into mature persons. By a strange "wrongness" we and our ancestors abused this gift of freedom and made the wrong choice. Of course, sometimes we have disregarded the laws of health through ignorance. Often, however, we have "gone wrong" and hurt our moral and physical health by wilful disobedience. But God, who is perfect Love, never gave us up, and never gives us up. Through responsive leaders such as Moses, God renewed His promise of wholeness:

"*If you will diligently hearken to the voice of the Lord your God, and do that*

which is right in his eyes, and give heed to his commandments and keep all his statutes, I will put none of the diseases upon you which I put upon the Egyptians;. for I am the Lord, your healer."
—Exodus 15 : 26

At the heart of the universe is the great and gracious Creator and loving Father of our spirits. He desires that each of us should realize what He said long ago: "*I am the Lord, your healer.*"

Through His chosen representatives, God transmitted His promise that He will take our sickness and failure upon Himself and will create the world anew. To see the picture God promises to make real for all who trust and serve Him and live by His rules of health, read chapter 35 of the Book of Isaiah. Read also the sublime words describing the One who is our healer and deliverer in Isaiah's fifty-third chapter.

GOD GAVE US CHRIST

God gave us the unsurpassed gift of His Son Jesus Christ that we might know His will for us in health and abundant life. Jesus Christ, perfectly human and uniquely divine, is the demonstration of God's purpose that all God's children should have radiant health. Jesus Himself said that this is why He came: "*I am come that they may have life, and have it abundantly.*" God wants you and every other human being to have and enjoy life; to have it in abundance, to the full, till it overflows. In His first public statement, Jesus said to the group gathered in His home "church" that the words of Isaiah, chapter 61, were fulfilled in His coming. This meant that in Christ the power of God to liberate human beings from the evils which had invaded their lives was present as in no other person. (Read Luke 4: 16–30.)

DISEASE IS THE ENEMY
CHRIST FIGHTS TO OVERCOME

Evil in any form is the demonic intruder in God's world. Christ Jesus came to destroy the works of the devil (1 John 3: 8). The devil's works include any form of sin and illness. Can we read of the healing ministry of Jesus and doubt that God's perfect will is for the well-being of His children? Whenever Jesus encountered sickness or disability in a person, He overcame it. Of course, the patients whom Jesus cured, of whom we read in the Gospels, were given more than what we call healing for their bodies. Jesus knew that the deepest sickness is sickness of soul. Therefore, He delivered men from their guilt; their sense of brokenness; their feelings of hostility, of meaninglessness, of rejection.

In Jesus Christ God's design for His family becomes clear and luminous. In Christ, God's power to liberate the captive, give sight to the blind, and deep healing for inner hurts is made manifest. Whether we are sick in the usual sense or well, each of us needs the deliverance, the salvation, the wholeness Christ offers.

As Jesus of Nazareth was in Palestine nineteen centuries ago, God is eternally. As Jesus taught and practised in Galilee, so the living Christ teaches and acts today in every community where His Holy Spirit is welcomed. He teaches that illness is an enemy, and He asks us to fight disease. He does more; He promises supernatural help in our struggle against sickness and pain. An experienced pastor wrote, "Whenever a patient declares war on his complaint and earnestly desires to get well, he can be sure that all the resources of Almighty God are on his side." What we call the healing forces of nature is God cooperating in the knitting of a broken bone, in the healing of a wound, in the marshalling of other forces in the body to defeat a virus or infection.

God wants you to be well in every part of your body-mind-soul personality. As Martin Luther translated Exodus 15: 26, God assures us, "*I am the Lord thy Physician.*"

Thine arm, O Lord, in days of old,
  Was strong to heal and save;
It triumphed o'er disease and death,
  O'er darkness and the grave.
To Thee they went, the blind, the dumb
  The palsied, and the lame,
The leper with his tainted life,
  The sick with fevered frame.

And lo! Thy touch brought life and health,
  Gave speech, and strength, and sight;
And youth renewed and frenzy calmed
  Owned Thee, the Lord of light:
And now, O Lord, be near to bless,
  Almighty as of yore,
In crowded street, by restless couch,
  As by Gennesaret's shore.

. . . .

Be Thou our great Deliverer still,
  Thou Lord of life and death;
Restore and quicken, soothe and bless,
  With Thine Almighty breath.
To hands that work and eyes that see,
  Give wisdom's heavenly lore,
That whole and sick, and weak and strong,
  May praise Thee evermore.
        —EDWARD HAYES PLUMPTRE

SCRIPTURE TO STRENGTHEN

My grace is sufficient for thee.
             —2 CORINTHIANS 12: 9 (KJ.)

He took our infirmities.
                        —MATTHEW 8: 17

Cast thy burden upon the Lord.
              —PSALM 55: 22 (KJ.)

My flesh and my heart faileth: but God is the strength of my heart, and my portion for ever.
            PSALM 73: 26 (KJ.)

As you read these passages, believe that God is speaking to you through the words of the Bible: Isaiah 35, Isaiah 53, Psalm 23, Luke 4: 16–30, Psalm 55, Matthew 11: 28–29.

ASSURANCES AND PRAYERS

Words to say to Christ whom having not seen with our physical eyes we may "see" with the eyes of faith:

Lord Jesus, I believe that I am loved

by Thee. I believe that Thou art near me and strong to help me. I believe that Thou art working even now in ways known to me and in ways unknown, to deliver me from every enemy of God's loving purpose.

I confess that I have sinned by ignoring or breaking God's laws of health; I confess to my doubt of God's reality and Thy power to save and guide and support all who trust Thee. Now I take God's gift of faith and receive Thy forgiveness.

Lord, I thank Thee for the healing Thou art giving to me even while I pray. May I show forth my thankfulness not in words only but in my calmness, my cheerfulness, my considerateness for others. Amen.

☩ ☩ ☩

Faith came singing into my room
  And other guests took flight,
Grief and anxiety, fear and gloom,
  Sped out into the night.

I wondered that such peace could be,
  But Faith said gently, "Don't you see
That they can never live with me?"
          —AUTHOR UNKNOWN

O Saviour Christ, our woes dispel;
  For some are sick, and some are sad,
And some have never loved Thee well,
  And some have lost the love they had;

And some are pressed with worldly care,
  And some are tried with sinful doubt;
And some such grievous passions tear
  That only Thou canst cast them out;

.   .   .   .

And none, O Lord, have perfect rest,
  For none are wholly free from sin;
And they who fain would serve Thee best
  Are conscious most of wrong within.

.   .   .   .

Thy touch has still its ancient power;
  No word from Thee can fruitless fall;
Hear, in this solemn evening hour,
  And in Thy mercy heal us all.
          —HENRY TWELLS

Heavenly Father, I would and do surrender all self-will and whatever would hinder Thy Healing Love; forgive my sins; cleanse my heart; guide me; strengthen me; give me peace of mind and healing sleep; fill me with healing virtue and make me whole; through Jesus Christ.—JOHN MAILLARD

II

ALL HEALING IS DIVINE

Bless the Lord, . . .
who heals all your diseases.
—PSALM 103: 3

Christians believe this Biblical affirmation, or they should. God loves us with an everlasting love, and seeks to give us life in its fullness. By our rebellion against His will and by our ignorance of His laws, we frustrate our heavenly Father's perfect plan. Moreover, apart from all we can discover about our failure to co-operate with God, sin and sickness seem to be invaders of God's territory. Everything we know about God from the Scripture—in the life, teaching, ministry, and in the death and resurrection of our Lord Jesus Christ—

convinces us that illness is an enemy which has no right in the universe at all. This is why we instinctively try to avoid hurting ourselves. This is why our brain seems to telegraph messages to every part of the body to save us from preventable pain. This is why we say "nature" helps so wonderfully in the knitting of broken bones and in the healing of wounds. The divine Physician, Jesus our Lord, met a woman suffering from what today we might call a curvature of the spine. He spoke to her as "*a woman who had had a spirit of infirmity for eighteen years; she was bent over and could not fully straighten herself. And when Jesus saw her, he called her and said to her, 'Woman, you are freed from your infirmity.' And he laid his hands upon her, and immediately she was made straight, and she praised God*" (Luke 13: 11–13).

In Jesus' action God was conquering the enemy disease. It is true that no human being ever heals another. All the human healer can do is to co-operate with God who alone heals. A French surgeon understood this truth and said, "I dressed the wound; God healed it."

Healing is spiritual because it comes from the divine Spirit who is our Maker. Redeemer, and Friend.

This affirmation of faith was written for patients in a hospital:

> We believe in God who is like a good Father.
> He is near to us and strong to help us.
> We believe our faith is a confident trust in the truth and goodness of God.
> We believe our hope is a power to fill the present and the future with deepest meaning.
> We believe our love is the means by which this faith will be made real in our lives.

THROUGH MANY WAYS

Does spiritual healing, sometimes called faith healing, mean that we must rely *only* on faith and prayer? No, because all healing is spiritual. True, some good people use the term "spiritual healing" to mean only the healing which follows the prayers of faith, or perhaps the laying on of hands by some person who seems to have the "*gifts of healing.*" But *all healing of our minds and bodies is spiritual*, because God the Holy Spirit is the source of all goodness. Another way to say it is to say that all healing is divine.

WHICH IS THE BEST WAY FOR GOD TO HEAL?

Many try to answer this question. Recall what was said about the healer needing to co-operate with the divine Physician. The patient, members of his family, and his friends must also co-operate to the best of their ability with the divine Physician. So we ask, "What is the most effective way of co-operating with God in this person's sickness or injury?" God uses different healing methods. Surgery, X-ray treatments, medicines, psychiatric counselling—all are used by God when employed by qualified persons.

In the booklet of worship services of the Iona Community of Scotland, these words precede the order for "The Divine Healing Service of Intercession for Sick Persons":

It is not true that there is "material healing" performed by doctors, while "spiritual" healing is performed by ministers and congregations. *All healing is spiritual.* The man who discovered penicillin was the last of a long chain of researchers. But in the whole process was the Hand of God. Again, in the patient work of nursing there is the Spirit of God. Wherever a sick person, by medical or surgical work and nursing, has been made well, he has been spiritually cured [by spiritual means]. Wherever health is restored, it means the laws of God have been recovered, applied and become operative.... You cannot divide off the spirit of a man from the body of a man. Thus, if all "material well-being" is due to spiritual forces, it means that we should call in the Spirit more than some of us do in all our material concerns.[2]

We pray with Charles Kingsley:

From Thee all skill and science flow,
  All pity, care, and love,
All calm and courage, faith and hope;
  O pour them from above.

DOCTORS ARE DIVINE HEALERS

In the Scriptures between the Old and the New Testaments, called the Books of the Apocrypha, there is a noble tribute to the physician which every Christian may endorse. It is found in the Book of Ecclesiasticus:

Honour a physician with the honour due unto him for the uses which ye may have of him: for the Lord hath created him. For of the most High cometh healing, and he shall receive honour of the king. The

28

skill of the physician shall lift up his head: and in the sight of great men he shall be in admiration.

The Lord hath created medicines out of the earth; and he that is wise will not abhor them. . . . And he hath given men skill, that he might be honoured in his marvellous works. With such doth he heal [men,] and taketh away their pains. . . .

My son, in thy sickness be not negligent: but pray unto the Lord, and he will make thee whole. Leave off from sin, and order thine hands aright, and cleanse thy heart from all wickedness. . . . Then give place to the physician, for the Lord hath created him: let him not go from thee, for thou hast need of him. There is a time when in their hands there is good success. For they shall also pray unto the Lord, that he would prosper that which they give for ease and remedy to prolong life.
—ECCLESIASTICUS 38: 1-7, 9-10,
12-14 (K.J.)

God uses skilful, conscientious physicians and surgeons even when they themselves are not conscious of God's presence nor of their vocation as one blessed and used by Him. In the Bible, the prophet Isaiah reports God as saying to Cyrus the pagan invader, "*I gird you, though you do not know me*" (Isaiah 45: 5). God thinks of Cyrus, who is not a professing believer in God, as one of His shepherds, carrying out a noble purpose. Many doctors are devout believers in God. All true physicians and surgeons have a deep reverence for life and for the Source of life. But whether they are aware of God and His use of them or not, such persons are God's agents and instruments.

Physicians speak of the healing power of nature. Whether we speak of Nature or of nature's God, God is the author of healing and the inspiration of the science of healing.

God uses many methods and persons to realize His loving purpose of restoration of our souls and bodies. We do well to thank Him for them, and to pray that each of this "team"—physician, surgeon, psychiatrist, nurse, chaplain, pastor, and all others dedicated to healing—may be anointed with His love and skill.

Father, whose will is life and good
   For all of mortal breath,
Bind strong the bond of brotherhood
   Of those who fight with death.

Empower the hands and hearts and wills
   Of friends in lands afar,
Who battle with the body's ills,
   And wage Thy holy war.

Where'er they heal the maimed and blind,
   Let love of Christ attend:
Proclaim the good Physician's mind,
   And prove the Saviour friend.
—HARDWICKE DRUMMOND RAWNSLEY

PRAYERS

FOR DOCTORS AND NURSES

Father of mercies and God of love, who hast made the body of man to be the temple of the Holy Spirit, be with all those who practise the art of healing,

that they may do so in the fear of Thee and according to the example of Him who healed the sick and raised the fallen; even Jesus Christ, our Lord. Amen.[3]
—From *Hospital Prayers*

FOR ALL ENGAGED IN HEALING

He . . . healed them.—LUKE 4: 40

Merciful God, we pray for all healers. For those to whom Thou hast given skill in surgery and medicine, we pray, asking that they may be wise, strong, and tender, and greatly used in curing disease.

For nurses we ask a high view of their calling, and patience and grace to assist effectively in restoration to health and cheerfulness in affliction.

For those who deal with mental illness, we pray that Thy Spirit may enlighten them with insight and power to bring peace to troubled minds.

For all to whom Thou hast given gifts of healing, and for Thy Church commissioned to heal, we beseech Thee that by these means Thy power and love may be shown forth. In the name of the great Physician of our bodies and souls, Jesus Christ. Amen.

—Adapted from an UNKNOWN AUTHOR

FOR RESEARCH WORKERS

Almighty God, with whom are hid the treasures of wisdom and knowledge, pour out Thy Spirit on all who are engaged in research. Give them hope, courage, and strength that they may labour faithfully to find out the secrets of nature. Impart to them an ever-increasing knowledge of Thy ways, that they may help to prevent disease and to restore health. Hasten the glad day when pain shall be no more and Thy rule of love shall fill the whole earth; through Jesus Christ, our Lord. Amen.[3]

—From *Hospital Prayers*

Eternal God our Father, who didst send Thy Son Jesus Christ to be the Saviour and healer of men, we pray

Thee to bless the selfless service of
doctors, nurses, and hospital workers
who show forth Thy love in action. We
thank Thee that through the uncovering
of the causes of disease and the secrets
of health, disease is being mastered and
Thy children are finding the abundant
life which Thou dost desire for us. In
the name and Spirit of Jesus Christ our
Lord we pray. Amen.
                              —DAVID A. MACLENNAN

A PSALM FOR THE HOSPITAL

The hospital is the Lord's
And the operating-rooms thereof.
The wards, and they that dwell therein,
For He hath founded it in loving kindness
And established it upon the mercy of
  Christ.
Who shall ascend unto the house of
  health?
Who shall serve in the holy place of
  healing?
He whose hands have been made surgic-
  ally clean

And in whose heart is the pure love of truth;
She who hath lifted up her heart unto service
And dedicated her life to the ministry of healing—
These shall receive the blessing.
They shall receive honours from the Lord.
They shall receive affection from all mankind.

—AUTHOR UNKNOWN

A BLESSING

May He who manifested Himself unto His people in the work of healing reveal Himself through all who tend the sick in the watches of the night. May He bless all who strive for healing of every disease and every infirmity among His people.

May His life-giving Spirit drive all fear from before us and keep us in His peace.

—From *Services for Broadcasting*

III

THE GREAT PHYSICIAN NOW IS NEAR

A "gospel hymn" declares a profound and timeless truth:

The Great Physician now is near,
The sympathizing Jesus.

Ever since God raised Jesus from the dead He has been within reach of those who need Him. Nineteen hundred years ago in Palestine He came to give salvation—healing and wholeness—to every child of God. On the first Good Friday He identified Himself with us in our sin and pain. In the words of a poet, all the world's anguish was forced through the channels of a single heart. Somehow through that agony of God in Christ on the cross God's own pardon and peace are offered to us. On the first Easter, He proclaimed and demonstrated the victory of life over death and of love over hatred. Easter was God's V-Day —Victory Day—for the human race: the day of God's victory over physical and spiritual death. Therefore, if we believe, as we do, that Jesus Christ was raised from the dead, then it means that He is alive today. If Jesus Christ is alive today, then the power of His risen life is available for us as truly as it was for the Apostle Peter and the other apostles immediately after His resurrection. Peter said, *"By the name of Jesus Christ of Nazareth, whom you crucified, whom God raised from the dead, by him this man is standing before you well."*

BY THE NAME OF JESUS

By the new powers God set free in Christ we may have newness of life. *"For if while we were enemies we were reconciled to God by the death of his Son, much more, now that we are reconciled, shall we be saved [daily delivered from sin's dominion] by his [resurrection] life.*" This salvation by Christ's resurrection life includes more than deliverance from sickness, yet it does include such deliverance or healing.

God was in Jesus Christ in His earthly life in Palestine. God was in Christ who died upon Calvary's cross. God was and is in the risen Lord. Therefore we worship and seek to serve not a Jesus who lived long ago and far away, but the living Christ. Our Lord Himself promised to be our Companion in every place and time: "*Lo, I am with you always....*" His first followers saw Him in His mysterious and yet familiar body after His resurrection. In His name and through His power they healed the sick and brought a new springtime into the wintry world of their time. They had seen Him victorious over death, and so they believed. But He Himself said, "*Blessed are those who have not seen and yet believe.*" We who have not seen Him except with "the eyes of faith" are blessed if we dare to believe that

Jesus Christ rose from the dead and that He is with us now. The cross is our most sacred symbol, but Christ is not on the cross now! Where is He? He is with us as no other person can be with us. He is with us as a Presence, even though we cannot see Him. When we call upon His name, we call upon Him, a Personality, a Presence.

HOW CHRIST COMES TO US

How the risen Lord saves us into newness of life and how He heals us is a mystery. The resurrection of Christ is surely, next to the fact of Christ, the supreme miracle of history. A Scottish theologian, the late Principal D. S. Cairns, once said, "The Resurrection is the land where the great mists lie, but it is the land from which the great rivers flow." The "great rivers" of divine power flow from the resurrection. In those "rivers" we find healing.

Yes, how Christ comes to us by our beds of pain or weakness is a mystery.

But He comes. All we need to do is to turn to Him in our need, seeking Him in loving trust. Always we must seek to know Christ first, not to seek first the "signs and wonders" we want Him to do for us. An old acrostic tells us the meaning of such faith in Him:

F orsaking	F eeling	F inding
A ll	A fraid	A nother
I	I	I
T ake	T rust	T ell
H im	H im	H im

To trust Him is to take Him at His word. To take Him at His word is to quietly say to oneself:

(1) *Christ stands beside me.* His healing power is even now entering into my body and mind and soul. Even as long ago He came to His disciples through closed doors behind which they were gathered fearfully (John 20: 19), so He can come into my very being, and fill me with His power, His peace, His life.

(2) *He is ready to forgive me* for ignoring and disobeying Him. When I

tell Him that I am truly sorry for any pain I have caused Him or any other person, He reaches out His hand in loving acceptance, "*Your sins are forgiven.*"

(3) *I will ask Him to make His presence known to me*, even though I cannot see Him or hear His voice. I will keep "turning" towards Him, for I know that such contact with His love and power is the secret of wholeness and health.

(4) When I feel too weak or depressed by some medication to do this for myself, or when I have too little faith, *I will ask my pastor or the hospital chaplain, or some friends to pray* for this contact with the Lord for me. I know that the prayers of others lift me into His presence.

(5) I know that Christ's healing love cannot operate if it is blocked by my resentment towards anyone. So *I will forgive all who may have hurt or wronged me*, and will let Christ's love flow through me to others.

(6) *I will take His Grace*—His unpurchasable loving help. I will rest on His

promise: "*I tell you, whatever you ask in prayer, believe that you receive it, and you will*" (Mark 11:24). Lord, I believe that I am receiving what Thou knowest I most need: Thy forgiveness, Thy peace at the centre of my being. Thy healing.

THE RISEN LORD WELCOMED

Where the Risen Lord is welcomed, there is peace;

Where the Risen Lord is trusted, there is freedom from guilt and fear;

Where the Risen Lord is followed and obeyed, there is power for living;

Where the Risen Lord is welcomed, trusted, obeyed, there is healing at the deepest level—even when the disease seems to resist all efforts to cure.

PRAYERS FOR HIS PRESENCE

Lord, who hast warned us that without thee we can do nothing; and by thy holy Apostle hast taught us that in thy strength we can do all things: So take and possess us, that our weakness may be transformed by thy power; that we be no longer our own, but thine; that it be not we who live, but thou who livest in us; who now reignest with the Father and the Holy Spirit, world without end.[4]

—From *Daily Prayer*

TRUST AND CONFIDENCE

Thou art my Lord and my God.

By Thy wounds I know that Thou art acquainted with grief and with suffering. By Thy Risen Presence with me I know that Thou hast conquered all in life and death that could make me fear.

I thank Thee, my Lord and my God, and I set out to face what lies ahead with new courage, peace and hope, knowing that in everything my hold on Thee will be strengthened, and that Thy hold on me will never slacken. Blessed be God through Jesus Christ my Saviour. Amen.[5]

—Jan Cowie

FOR TIMES OF PAIN

Lord Jesus, who in all the agony of the Cross didst remain more than conqueror, grant me a portion of Thy Spirit. By Thy Love Thou didst turn Thy suffering to use in the Salvation of the world. So may I be purified in this fire of suffering.

By Thy Love Thou didst take thought for Thy fellow-sufferers and Thy dear ones. So keep my spirit strong and unselfish. Then, O Lord, when I have mastered it, drive out my pain and weakness by Thy Lifegiving Spirit. Amen.[5]

—Jan Cowie

WE COMMEND UNTO THEE

We commend unto Thee, O Lord,
   our souls and our bodies,
   our minds and our thoughts,
   our prayers and our hopes,
   our health and our work,
   our life and our death,
our parents and brothers and sisters,
   our benefactors and friends,
     our neighbours, our countrymen,
     and all Christian folk
       this day and always.
          —LANCELOT ANDREWES

Christ with me, Christ before me,
Christ behind me, Christ within me,
Christ beneath me, Christ above me,
Christ at my right, Christ at my left,
  . . . .

Christ in the heart of every man who thinks of me,
Christ in the mouth of every man who speaks to me,
Christ in every eye that sees me,
Christ in every ear that hears me.
         —Attributed to ST. PATRICK

Thanks be to Thee, my Lord Jesus Christ,
For all the benefits Thou hast won for me,
For all the pains and insults Thou hast borne for me.
O most merciful Redeemer, Friend, and Brother,
May I know Thee more clearly,
Love Thee more dearly,
And follow Thee more nearly:
For ever and ever.
—RICHARD OF CHICHESTER

IV

WHEN GOD SEEMS TO SAY "NO"

If God is like Jesus, why does He not heal all who are sick and who trust Him and pray for healing? Is it because God is good but not almighty, or almighty and not good? Ever since human beings could think about deep matters, the problem of undeserved suffering has perplexed them. When we are in good health, it is easier than when we are sick to sing, "Teach me the patience of unanswered prayer." What are we to make of such prayers?

We believe that Jesus meant it when He taught that anything we ask in His name, our heavenly Father will grant us. To ask in His name means to ask for that which is in harmony with Christ's character and will. Surely to heal the sick, to give life to the dying, is in harmony with Jesus Christ's purpose and the kind of deliverance He wants for all God's children.

There have been miraculous answers to prayer for the critically ill. Equally sincere and fervent prayers for the recovery of health of someone much loved and needed seem to have gone unanswered.

SINCERE PRAYERS ANSWERED

Christians claim all sincere prayers are answered. Does this mean that God answers some of our prayers by saying what seems to be "No"? Yes. One of Christ's most faithful followers, the Apostle Paul, wrote of his prayers for healing, for deliverance from what he called his thorn in the flesh. Here is how the modern translation by J. B. Phillips gives Paul's account:

. . . I was given a physical handicap —one of Satan's angels—to harass me and

effectually stop any conceit. Three times I begged the Lord for it to leave me, but his reply has been, "My grace is enough for you: for where there is weakness, my power is shown the more completely." Therefore, I have cheerfully made up my mind to be proud of my weaknesses, because they mean a deeper experience of the power of Christ; I can even enjoy weaknesses, suffering, privations, persecutions and difficulties for Christ's sake. For my very weakness makes me strong in Him.[1]

Paul was sure that God answered his prayer, although at first it seemed as if God said "No." Certainly God did not give him the cure he pleaded to be given. As far as we know the great ambassador of Christ had to live all his years with the "thorn." When God seems to say "No" to our prayer for complete recovery of health, He may be saying "No" to one prayer in order to say a glorious "Yes" to the prayer we should have offered.

(1) Here, then, is wisdom from Christ and from His faithful disciples across the

centuries: *We must ask for what we believe to be His will for us, and above all ask that we may receive His grace to make us equal to anything that comes.* Grace is one of the loveliest and most meaningful words in the Bible. Grace is divine energy flowing towards us as the incoming ocean tide flows towards the shore. Grace is God's unpurchasable, loving help which enables us to stand anything that happens to us and to change it into something strong and useful. In 1 Peter 4: 10, we read of the many-coloured grace of God. A wise Christian scholar says this is a tremendous thought: it means that there is no colour in our human situation which the grace of God cannot match. We may be enjoying the gold of radiant health and success, or enduring the sombre black of pain or sorrow. In God's grace there is that which can meet and answer anything in our experience. When we pray that God may give us His grace whether He answers our prayer for healing "Yes" or "No," we are asking that we may trust Him to do for us and in us and through us what perfect Love desires to do.

He knows, He loves, He cares,
Nothing this truth can dim;
He always keeps the best for those
Who leave the choice to Him.

(2) When God seems to deny our prayers, we must remember that it is not because our faith is weak and our trust in Him inadequate. True, "*According to your faith be it done to you*" remains a valid principle. Faith clears the channels for divine power to flow in and through the human body and personality. But when healing does not come as we hope, or as soon as we hope, it does not mean that we have "not believed enough." Many heroic sufferers have been men and women of robust and radiant faith in God. There are sick persons who are more convincing witnesses to the power and love of Christ than many healthy people.

A Bible verse says that "*the saints will judge the world.*" Certainly the saints—those who put their trust in Christ and live the life of trust and love—manage their burdens of sickness or other disability better than those who have not joined Christ's company of friends. Dr. James Moffatt translated one verse as "*the pain God is allowed to guide.*" When we let God guide our pain, and guide us in handling our own pain or weakness, then God is healing us deep down in our souls even when we think healing of the body is delayed. In a story of a French Christian, *The Diary of a Country Priest* by Georges Bernanos, the doctor tells the saintly pastor that he has cancer of the stomach. At first the pastor is bewildered. Then he says:

Dear God, I give You all, willingly. But I don't know how to give, I just let them take. The best is to remain quiet. Because though I may not know how to give, You know how to take.... Yet I would have wished to be, once, just once, magnificently generous to You![6]

How can we be generous to God?

By trusting His knowledge of our need and of His love for us, rather than by trusting our knowledge of Him and our love for Him.

God answers prayers: sometimes, when hearts are weak,
He gives the very gifts believers seek,
But often faith must learn a deeper rest,
And trust God's silence when He does not speak;
For He whose name is Love will send the best.
Stars may burn out, nor mountain walls endure,
But God is true, His promises are sure
For those who seek.
—AUTHOR UNKNOWN

(3) When God seems to say "No" to prayers for physical healing, *He often heals the heart that is poisoned by guilt or resentment.* God heals the hurt caused by estrangement between the patient and a member of his family, or with one who was formerly a friend. Our Lord

Jesus said to the paralysed man first, not "You are healed," but "*Your sins are forgiven.*" In 2 Samuel 13: 2, we read, "*Ammon was so upset by his passion . . . that it made him ill*" (Moffatt). An eminent physician said that a bodily disease which we look upon as whole and entire in itself may, after all, be but a symptom of some ailment in the spiritual part. Of course it is also true that what we think is entirely mental or emotional may have a physical basis. But hate, guilt, or unchristian fear does upset our whole system. We all know how worry and grief and a sense of our moral failure can make us actually sick. Bad temper can literally prevent us from "seeing straight" and affect our physical vision. A physician said to Dr. E. Stanley Jones, "If three quarters of my patients found God, they would be well."

Divine healing takes place often when the Holy Spirit is allowed to make the sick person forgiving, loving, brave. A mature Christian woman who lives in Europe wrote these words:

"I have personally been given (in the full sense of that word) the certainty that if we pray to God to manifest his glory and leave him free to do so in his own way, then he will without fail do something—and will at the same time open our eyes that we may see in what he does the glorification of his name."[7]

—DOROTHEE HOCH

(4) When God seems to say "No" to us when we ask Him to cure us or one for whom we pray, *He gives us grace that we may use the suffering in ways which may seem mysterious or unbelievable to us.* St. Paul makes what seems a strange statement in writing to the Colossian Christians: "*I am suffering now on your behalf, but I rejoice in that; I would make up the full sum of all that Christ has to suffer in my person on behalf of the church, his Body*" (Moffatt). Here is the Christian's secret of radically changing pain and weakness into something beautiful: *offer the aches and pains, the sickness and anguish to God for the redemption of others.* When we do this,

somehow the wounds and pains are linked with Christ's suffering which He endured for the sake of all mankind. Then we enter into the royal fellowship of Christ's cross. This may seem baffling and strange, but it is true that those who take their share of hardship, who enter into the fellowship of Christ's suffering, experience also the power of His resurrection.

GOD ALWAYS HEALS

(5) Does that declaration make sense after what we have said concerning unanswered prayers, or prayers that seem answered by "No"? "God always heals," said a Christian psychologist who devoted many years to helping others find their way to victorious living. "God always cures," he said; "and sometimes His ultimate cure is the resurrection." E. Stanley Jones, in *Abundant Living*, says, "To some He entrusts the ministry of suffering until the Day of the Final Cure—the resurrection—in the

meantime giving them power, not merely to bear the suffering, but to use it."

Physical death comes to all, although we must not say glibly that any person's bodily death is God's perfect will. No one may speak with complete authority here, except the Lord of life and death; yet may we not say that sometimes God's cure is physical death followed by resurrection into life eternal? We must leave the issue with God.

Distraught parents of a desperately ill girl sent for their minister. This minister believed in spiritual healing. He regularly and carefully conducted private services for the healing of the sick. He came to the home, talked with the young woman who was critically ill, prayed with her parents. The sick girl found Christ; and He gave her His deep, unbreakable peace. It was the peace of God which passes understanding and also the peace of God which comes *with* understanding. She was reconciled to life and to death. She was reconciled to members of her family circle from whom she had been estranged. Her parents were healed of their fear of death and delivered from the haunting feeling that they were being punished by God through the illness of their child. A short time after these spiritual results took place, the daughter died. Is it not true to say that she was healed, as were her parents, before her physical death? May it not be true that her physical death was God's cure for her "incurable" sickness?

A deep believer in God's love and healing power, Ruth Robison, was asked, "How do you know that it is right to pray for a person who is seriously ill? How do you know that it is not time for this one to go?" Her answer was one of singular insight: "I don't presume to know when the time will come for you or anyone else to die, but this I do know, that you need not die sick. You can die well."[8]

Lord, it belongs not to my care,
    Whether I die or live;
To love and serve Thee is my share,
    And this Thy grace must give.

If life be long, I will be glad,
　That I may long obey;
If short—yet why should I be sad
　To soar to endless day?

Christ leads me through no darker rooms
　Than He went through before;
He that into God's kingdom comes,
　Must enter by this door.

. . . . . .

My knowledge of that life is small,
　The eye of faith is dim;
But 'tis enough that Christ knows all,
　And I shall be with Him.
　　　　　　—RICHARD BAXTER

Lord Jesus,
　draw me to Thyself by Thy heart of love;
　draw me to Thyself by Thy words of compassion;
　draw me to Thyself by the lonely agony of Thy suffering upon the Cross.
Grant that I may so know Thee as to find comfort in sorrow, and faith in darkness; and draw me ever closer to Thyself until, where sorrow and sighing

flee away, I see Thee in Thy heaven.
For Thy Name's sake I ask it. Amen.[9]
—MAURICE WOOD

PRAYER FOR GOD'S PRESENCE

Thou who art the source of all our strength, both in body and in soul, look mercifully upon thy servant, bearing in *his* body the pain of illness and in *his* soul the dark shadows of that burden which the weakened flesh must throw upon it. Be with *him* and let thy lovingkindness be known to *him*, both by day and in the longer hours of the night. May the everlasting arms hold *him* in quiet trust and comfort *him* against all loneliness and darkness. With the healing of thy spirit and the compassion of Christ's presence bring *him* to health again that we may rejoice in *his* life and in thy goodness. Amen.[10]
—SAMUEL H. MILLER

Father of all mercy, Shepherd of every hope, the Refuge of our bewildered hearts, steady us with thy most tender mercy lest the darkness of this hour hide the providences of a lifetime from our sight. Within the shadow of our fears thy love doth stand waiting upon the very threshold of our need. Though we cannot see the way, guide us step by step and strengthen us for each day's journey with a peace beyond our making. Wherever we walk, in sunshine or in shadow, show us the sign of Christ our Lord, who hath gone before us and suffered all things that we might be delivered from fear and in every extremity trust thee with our life. Amen.[10]

—SAMUEL H. MILLER

PRAYER FOR THE DYING

We lift up our hearts, O Lord, for the dying: for those who now can see the gate into the garden of deliverance and long to pass through it and find peace. If they have felt unwanted on earth, may they feel doubly welcomed as the gate opens. If they are distressed at leaving dear ones, especially little ones, may they know that they will be able to help from the other side and that everlasting arms of purpose and of love enclose all souls.

So may all fear of death pass away in a sense of wonder and joy as a new life begins, fairer and more satisfying than earth could ever show. May the utter contentment of those who trust Love, fill the hearts of all who are dying and may their souls rest in peace. For Thy name's sake. Amen.[11]

—LESLIE D. WEATHERHEAD

V

WHEN IT HURTS TERRIBLY

What can we do when an illness or injury causes us great pain? We can ask for a sedative. One of the great benefits of living today is that scientific research has made available safe and effective medicine to deaden pain. But sometimes our particular trouble brings pain in spite of anything the doctor or nurse may be able to do. It may be desirable for our ultimate healing that we endure some pain. It may be that we cannot tolerate certain drugs which other persons may take without any so-called "side effects."

Jesus is our great helper when the pain becomes almost unbearable. He was acquainted with suffering whether it came from bereavement (remember how He wept when He learned that His friend Lazarus had died), the hostility of men, the misunderstanding of His family, or the agony of death by crucifixion. The very word *excruciating* has a cross at the centre of it. It reminds us of how greatly Jesus suffered that we might have forgiveness, healing, and life eternal. Always during His earthly career our Lord Jesus heard "The still, sad music of humanity." The leper, the blind, the deaf, the chronic sufferer, the widow weeping out her heart moved Him to compassion. Is this not why we can sing,

There is no place where earth's sorrows
Are more felt than in heaven,

in the heart of our blessed Lord? He never denied the reality of pain. Pain to Him was as real as the nails driven into His quivering flesh when they nailed Him to a cross. He fought against pain, for He saw it to be part of that realm of evil He came to overthrow. Whenever He could, Jesus delivered persons from suffering. By the power of His Spirit Christ does so still. How can He help us when the pain becomes sharp?

BRING IT TO HIM

(1) *He helps us bear the pain by asking us to bring it to Him.* Just as in Mark's story of the epileptic lad and his father, we are to say to the divine Physician: "*Teacher, I brought my son to you . . . if you can do anything, have pity on us and help us*" (Mark 9: 17, 22). Christ says to us, although we may never hear His actual voice, "*If you can ! All things are possible to him who believes.*" Will you say to the Lord as if He stood beside you, "Master, I bring my pain to you . . . have pity . . . help me"? Only now you know that He is the crucified and risen Lord. He has suffered excruciating pain. God gave Him grace to bear His cross; He will give you grace to bear yours.

ASK GOD TO USE IT

(2) Another way Christ helps us is to show us that *we must accept the pain, and pray that somehow it may be used by God to further His good purposes*. We may not understand why we must suffer as we do. Nevertheless, we can bring the suffering to God. Only once did Jesus ask God "Why?" Then it was on the cross in His last hours. His moment of black despair brings Him closer to us in our despair. Quickly the feeling of forsakenness was replaced by one of trust: "*Father, into thy hands I commit my spirit!*" To accept our pain or weakness and to turn it over to the Christlike God who does not willingly afflict any of His children is to find relief and support. A gifted woman named Katherine Mansfield suffered from recurring illness for a long time. She was cured only by death. It is not certain how much of Katherine Mansfield's wisdom and courage came from Christian faith. But she was "*not far from the kingdom.*" She was young in

years when she wrote these unusual words:

"Suffering is boundless, it is eternity. One pang is eternal torment. . . . What must one do? There is no question of what is called 'passing beyond it.' This is false.

One must *submit*. Do not resist. Take it. Be overwhelmed. Accept it fully. Make it *part of life*.

Everything in life that we really accept undergoes a change. So suffering must become Love. This is the mystery. This is what I must do. I must pass from personal love to greater love. I must give to the whole of life what I gave to one. The present agony will pass—if it doesn't kill. It won't last. Now I am like a man who has had his heart torn out—but—bear it—bear it! As in the physical world, so in the spiritual world, pain does not last forever. It is only so terribly acute now. . . .

. . . If 'suffering' is not a repairing process, I will make it so. I will learn the lesson it teaches. These are not idle words. These are not the consolations of the sick.

Life is a mystery. The fearful pain will fade. I must turn to work. I must put my agony into something, change it. 'Sorrow shall be changed into joy.'

It is to lose oneself more utterly, to love more deeply, to feel oneself part of life,—not separate.

Oh Life! accept me—make me worthy —teach me."[12]

—KATHERINE MANSFIELD

You pray, "O God! accept me—help me to accept my pain—make me worthy of this compliment You have paid me by trusting me with this trouble—teach me what You want me to learn that the pain may not be wasted."

CHRIST IS MASTER OF PAIN

(3) When you and I do this, we learn *Christ is the Master of pain.* He gives deliverance. "*God shall wipe away all tears from their eyes; and there shall be*

no more death, neither sorrow, nor crying, neither shall there be any more pain: for the former things are passed away" (Revelation 21: 4. KJ.). But this wonderful promise shall not be fulfilled here —not completely. Tears, stabbing pains, sorrows may remain. But when we accept them *"for Christ's sake"* and our own growth in spiritual maturity, the power of such things is broken. The Gospel of Mark in the story of the tormented boy says that Christ cast out the spirit of evil behind the boy's agony. He does this still. When He touches our spirits with His spirit, when He expels the demons of selfcentredness, of resentment, or rebelliousness, of doubts, we draw closer to the time when *"there shall be no more pain."* Meanwhile, God is in it with us; and we find it is true in deeper ways than we can express that *"with his stripes we are healed."* One wrote: "It is as though God said, in the day of darkness, 'Here, my child, is something you can do for Me! Here is your little share in the burden which I have been carrying from the foundation of the world and must carry till the day break and the shadows flee. Here is your part with Me in the age-long cross I bear.'" Have you not noticed that those who are most helpful to others in their sufferings are often persons who have suffered deeply themselves? Pain can be transmuted into power. Bringing our pain to God in Christ, asking Him for help to accept it, praying Him to help us use it for His good purpose, may even bring us to say with the great Apostle: "*Most gladly therefore will I rather glory in my infirmities, that the power of Christ may rest upon me*" (2 Corinthians 12: 9. KJ.).

PRAYERS

WE OFFER OUR GIFT OF PAIN

O Thou who didst gather up into Thyself on Calvary the sorrow of all the world, and whose heart was pierced by many deadly spears, to Thee we offer our gift of pain, that, united with Thy redemptive suffering, it may be sanctified

for the healing of the wounds of men.
For Thy love's sake. Amen.

O Jesus Christ who endured the agony of body and mind which crucifixion brought, Thou didst bear Thy cross: help me to bear my pain. Amen.

✠ ✠ ✠

O Love Divine! that stoop'st to share
  Our sharpest pang, our bitterest tear,
On Thee we cast each earth-born care,
  We smile at pain while Thou art near!

． ． ． ． ． ． ． ．

On Thee we cast our burdening woe,
  O Love Divine, forever dear,
Content to suffer while we know,
  Living and dying, Thou art near!
         —Oliver Wendell Holmes

O Joy that seekest me through pain,
  I cannot close my heart to Thee;
I trace the rainbow through the rain,
And feel the promise is not vain
  That morn shall tearless be.

O Cross that liftest up my head,
  I dare not ask to fly from Thee;
I lay in dust life's glory dead,
And from the ground there blossoms red
  Life that shall endless be.
—GEORGE MATHESON

THE PEACE OF PAIN

There is a peace which no men know
Save those whom suffering hath laid low
    The peace of pain.

A strength, which only comes to those
Who've borne defeat—greater, God knows,
    Than victory.

A happiness which comes at last,
After all happiness seems past,
    The joy of peace.
—AUTHOR UNKNOWN

Father, if He, the Christ, were Thy Revealer,
  Truly the First Begotten of the Lord,

Then must Thou be a Suff'rer and a Healer,
  Pierced to the heart by the sorrow of the sword.

. . . .

Peace does not mean the end of all our striving,
  Joy does not mean the drying of our tears;
Peace is the power that comes to souls arriving
  Up to the light where God Himself appears.

. . . .

Give me, for light, the sunshine of Thy sorrow,
  Give me, for shelter, shadow of Thy Cross;
Give me to share the glory of Thy morrow,
  Gone from my heart the bitterness of Loss.[13]

—G. A. STUDDERT-KENNEDY

A PRAYER TO ACCEPT PAIN

In the quietness of the evening hour,
In the stillness of the night,
In the freshness of the morning,
The strength of early day,
Good Lord, hear my prayer. . . .

Make me well and strong.
I rest in Thee, Thy healing power within,
I rest in Thy sure support
And Thou dost make me whole.
As the shepherd watches the sheep,
In green pastures and beside still waters;

As Thy creatures lie down to rest,
So I trust Thee and Thy healing force;
O God, I will trust Thee.
Carry away the pain, the restlessness;
I am at rest;
Take from me the heated moments
And let me be at peace. . . .

"My peace I give unto you," said Jesus.
That peace I seek,
The peace of him who walked beside the sea,

Who healed the sick and comforted the sad,
Heal Thou me, O God, and let me be at peace.
Comfort Thou my loved ones and give them ease. . . .
Amen. . . . Give me rest and quiet. . . . Amen and amen.[14]

—RUSSELL L. DICKS

VI

Deep Peace Helps God Heal Us

A small boy I knew had his first experience of illness. He was asked to describe how he felt, and where it hurt most. This was his diagnosis: "A fuss bust loose in my head!" He was enduring his first headache. Human beings of all ages and backgrounds know what it means to have a "fuss bust loose" in head or heart, or in some other part of the body-mind God has given us. Three out of four persons suffer from anxiety, reported an American psychiatrist to a world convention of medical specialists. Anxiety gnaws away at our inner serenity; and when anxiety is joined by fear, our health may be hurt or our cure delayed. Christ has taught us to believe that our bodies, through which our personalities must function, are temples of God's spirit. If within this temple of the soul there are dark intruders—anxiety, fear, guilt feelings, moral weakness, spiritual insecurity—Christ offers help. "He is able" to make us more than conquerors. This is the victorious cry of the New Testament Christians and of Christians in every era since the New Testament was written. Where Christ enters and is given His rightful place as Lord and Master the evil tenants are expelled. God's deep peace will then guard our hearts and minds in Christ Jesus, so that no enemy may return as a lodger.

HOW DO WE EXPERIENCE GOD'S PEACE?

(1) First, we must face ourselves and the actions, thoughts, or conditions which have made us anxious, afraid, depressed, or feel guilty. Certainly the complete examination and various tests

which qualified persons in a medical centre can provide are essential. Only so can we discover any organic cause of our "dis-ease" and discomfort. It is as foolish to rely only on prayer and "purely spiritual" healing as it is to rely only on medicines, surgery, or other scientific means of healing.

(2) Diagnosis of our condition having been made and treatment prescribed by our physician or surgeon, we place ourselves confidently in the doctor's hands. He is one of God's instruments of healing. But what if inward peace still eludes us? Then *we must face our inner selves with Christ*. Self-examination may be necessary to uncover the causes of our uneasiness. We may need to face the wrongs we have done, the relationships with others we have broken which need to be mended with Christ's help. Christ wants us to get into harmony with God who loves us. The Master knows that we cannot do this unless we achieve harmony with those from whom we are separated by misunderstanding, grudges, jealousy, or other sins of the spirit.

Having faced ourselves and the worst about ourselves, we then turn our sins and failures over to Christ that He may forgive us. Dr. Leslie D. Weatherhead wrote, "The forgiveness of God, in my opinion, is the most powerful therapeutic idea in the world." No one can measure the immense streams of healing energy which flow from realizing the truth of John's words: "*The blood [that is, the life] of Jesus Christ his Son cleanses us from all sin.*" Peace that passes all understanding comes from realizing God's pardon.

(3) Accepting God's acceptance of us through realizing His forgiveness and love, *we then learn to be content with whatever may be His will or plan for us.* Because Christ is our truest picture of God, we know that God's will is for our highest and richest life. Then we say, not in pious or sullen resignation, but joyfully and hopefully, "*Thy will be done.*" God does not want us always to be contented with what happens to us. Christ resisted disease and other forms of evil. So must we. Nor are we to

resign ourselves to what we ought to fight. Instead of rebellion and easy resignation, we are to work with God for our redemption. As we open ourselves to God's love and co-operate with His good purpose, we may expect to know the peace of God which comes even in the midst of difficulty and distress, which like the "eye" of a storm has peace at the heart of seemingly endless agitation.

(4) A fourth proven road to God's peace is *the way of prayer*. We must never prescribe for God! We must never tell Him what to do, but we have a right o pray for anything which it is right to ask of One who is more like the best father we can imagine than like anyone else.

How shall we pray?

Pray affirmatively, as you believe Jesus our Lord would want you to pray. Others have found these Christian affirmations helpful. Say them as if Christ were seated beside you:

"In Christ I am one with the divine Power.

"In Christ I am one with the Love which understands and forgives.

"In Christ I am one with the Peace that passeth understanding.

"In Christ I am one with unlimited resources.

"In Christ I have power over opposing conditions such as fear, lack of confidence, difficult circumstances.

"In Christ I am one with His patience, purity, joy, wisdom, and contentment."

Pray frequently in words of Scripture such as you will find at the end of this chapter, or in your own words. This kind of prayer is an act of commitment. You may say: "Quietly, confidently, peacefully, I confide myself and my needs, my dear ones, this moment and always into Thy keeping, O Lord." Or: "Father, into Thy hands I commend my spirit and my body, believing that even now Thou art doing for me and for all who trust Thee, exceeding abundantly above all that I can ask or think."

(5) Another cure for anxiety is to *practise God's presence by repeating to yourself the great passages of the Bible.* Some of these are given elsewhere in this book. Personalize them if it helps by

changing the pronouns in the Bible verses, as has been done in these:

As my days, so shall my strength be.
—DEUTERONOMY 33:25 (KJ.)

In quietness and confidence shall be my strength.—ISAIAH 30:15 (KJ.)

Thou wilt keep me in perfect peace whose mind is stayed on Thee, because I trust in Thee.—ISAIAH 26:3 (KJ.)

His grace is sufficient for me; for his strength is made perfect in [my] weakness.
—2 CORINTHIANS 12:9 (KJ.)

CHRISTIAN AFFIRMATIONS

Say the words of this old German choral to yourself:

In His arms I rest me,
Foes that would molest me
   Cannot reach me there.
Though the earth be shaking,
Every heart be quaking,
   God dispels our fear.

Sin and Hell in conflict fell,
With their deadliest darts assail us,
Jesus will not fail us.

THEN WHAT ARE WE AFRAID OF?

During World War I, men were engaged in the extremely dangerous task of mine sweeping in the waters surrounding the British Isles. They found freedom from fear of sudden and violent death by practising the presence of God. Before setting out, the skipper of one of the British trawler patrols introduced a simple and impressive tradition on his ship. The men gathered around their captain at the wheel and held a one-minute service:

Skipper: Are we all here?
Men: All of us here under God's care. Amen.
Skipper: Then what are we afraid of?
Men: We are afraid of nothing. Amen.

You and I can have such confidence. God's seas are great, our boats are small, but if "All of us [are] here under God's care," so let it be (Amen). "*Therefore we will not fear.*"

"*Be still, and know that I am God.*"
—PSALM 46: 10

*He makes me lie down in green pastures.
He leads me beside still waters;
He restores my soul [my life].*
—PSALM 23: 2–3

Deep peace of the running wave to you,
Deep peace of the flowing air to you,
Deep peace of the quiet earth to you,

. . . .

Deep peace of the flock of stars to you,
Deep peace of the Son of Peace to you.
—FIONA MACLEOD

ASK AND RECEIVE

Ask, and it will be given you; seek and you will find; knock, and it will be opened to you. For every one who asks receives, and he who seeks finds, and to him who knocks it will be opened.

—MATTHEW 7: 7–8

GOD IS YOUR GUARDIAN

He who dwells in the shelter of the Most High,
who abides in the shadow of the Almighty,
Will say to the Lord, "My refuge and my fortress;
my God, in whom I trust."
For he will deliver you from the snare of the fowler
and from the deadly pestilence;
He will cover you with his pinions,
and under his wings you will find refuge;
his faithfulness is a shield and buckler.

—PSALM 91: 1–4

The Lord will keep you from all evil;
he will keep your life.
The Lord will keep
your going out and your coming in
from this time forth and for evermore.

—PSALM 121: 7–8

Have no anxiety about anything, but in everything by prayer and supplication with thanksgiving let your requests be made known to God. And the peace of God, which passes all understanding, will keep [shall garrison and mount guard over] your hearts and your minds in Christ Jesus.—PHILIPPIANS 4: 6–7

*They who wait for the Lord
shall renew their strength.*

ISAIAH 40: 31

CHRIST'S CURE FOR WORRY

"Therefore I tell you, do not be anxious about your life, what you shall eat or what you shall drink, nor about your body what you shall put on. Is not life more than food, and the body more than clothing? Look at the birds of the air: they neither sow nor reap nor gather into barns, and yet your heavenly Father feeds them. Are you not of more value than they? And which of you by being anxious can add one cubit to his span of life?"

—MATTHEW 6: 25–27

LIVE ONE DAY AT A TIME

"*And why are you anxious about clothing? Consider the lilies of the field, how they grow; they neither toil nor spin; yet I tell you, even Solomon in all his glory was not arrayed like one of these. But if God so clothes the grass of the field, which today is alive and tomorrow is thrown into the oven, will he not much more clothe you, O men of little faith? Therefore do not be anxious, saying, 'What shall we eat?' or 'What shall we drink?' or 'What shall we wear?' For the Gentiles [pagans] seek all these things; and your heavenly Father knows that you need them all. But seek first his kingdom and his righteousness, and all these things shall be yours as well.*

"*Therefore do not be anxious about tomorrow, for tomorrow will be anxious for itself. Let the day's own trouble be sufficient for the day.*"

—MATTHEW 6:28–34

SUGGESTIONS FOR PRAYER IN TIME OF ILLNESS

WHEN YOU ARE SICK

O God, Thou art my Maker; Thou art the Sustainer of my life; Thou art Love. And I am Thine; my life is in Thy care; I know Thy will for me is good. In this illness, enable me to be receptive to all help: the wise counsel of the doctor, the tender care of my loved ones (name them). Keep me free from worry and uneasiness. Help me to place full trust in Thee and those who minister in Thy name. Help me to be "healthy" in mind and feelings. And may I be truly receptive to Thy healing powers as they flow through the deep places of my personality. May Thy Spirit work freely in me: may I not prevent Thee in any way; may I yield myself unreservedly to Thee.

Above all, help me to use this occasion in accord with Thy will: for the final good of my soul, and in such a way as to be helpful to all who are concerned for me.

Whatever may be the outcome, help me to witness to Thy love and care:

Whether to be healed, may I receive this blessing gratefully;
Whether to bear pain, may I do so bravely;
Whether to suffer limitations, may I do so patiently and gladly;
Whether to live or to die, to do all to Thy glory, knowing that Thou dost care for me now and for eternity.[15]

—CHESTER A. PENNINGTON

WHEN ANOTHER IS SICK

O God, Giver of life, Source of all true strength, I pray for ———.

May (he) trust (himself) to Thy care: with faith in those who are tending (him); with knowledge of our concern and prayers; with complete assurance of Thy love for (him).

May (he) know that Thou art always

with (him). Give (him) a sense of Thy healing presence and power. Help (him) to yield (himself) completely to Thy Spirit, as Thou dost strive to work in (him) even now. Free (him) from worry and fretting; may (he) truly trust Thee.

Enable us who care for (him) to preserve an attitude of faith and trust. Keep us from being tense and worried; so that our feelings will not disturb (him), but will sustain (him) and give courage, hope and strength.

May our love and concern be deeply and truly communicated to (him). May we show it every way we can . . . may Thy Spirit minister to (him) in the depths of (his) heart, carrying love, support, confidence.

Grant (him) the assurance that Thou wilt work with (him), in this and every time of need, for (his) truest good, both here and in eternity.[15]

—CHESTER A. PENNINGTON

A PRAYER CONCERNING HOPE

O Thou God, Source of hope and hopefulness,
Thou who hast sought to give us hope
And to strengthen us for the day's task,
We are quiet before Thee.
We give over the tensions that have claimed us
And the anxieties that have driven us;
We repent of the heated moments and the restless nights that have beset us.
Strong desires, strong passions, strong ambitions,
These combine to enslave us.
We are reflective; we lift our eyes to the hills;
We give over ourselves to the sure support of nature about us;
We rest in the faith of yesterday and wait for the return of hope.
Turn not Thy face from us, O God of our trust—
Forgive us our trespasses and make us whole again,
Through Jesus Christ our Lord. Amen.[14]

—Russell L. Dicks

A PRAYER TO RECOVER HOPE

O God, Thou who didst create us and bring us forth,
Thou who dost love us with an eternal love,
Give us quietness of spirit and ease of hurt.
Forgive us, O God, for those things that we so deeply regret, real or imagined,
Make us strong to correct those things that can be corrected,
And reward those we have offended.
May we know that in our hearts we are sorry for the hurt we have brought them.
O God, lift Thou our spirits from despair,
Give us rest and relaxation,
Open our minds to a healing of the spirit,
And give us a sense of the meaningfulness of life.
May we again hear the birds sing, the voices of little children,
May we feel the warmth of the sun and the cool of the night.
May we know again the warmth of human affection,

And give us a vision to see life as it is:
steady, whole, hopeful,
Through Jesus Christ our Lord. Amen.[14]
—Russell L. Dicks

FOR CHRIST'S BLESSING

O Lord Jesus Christ, to whom all the sick were brought that they might be healed, and who didst send none of them away without Thy blessing; look in compassion upon all who come to Thee for healing of heart and soul and body; send them not away without Thy blessing, but now and evermore grant them Thy grace. Amen.
—Adapted from a prayer by
G. H. Sharpe

O God, Giver of life and Fountain of health, heal the hurts of our hearts and the ills of our bodies by the power of Thy cleansing and renewing grace. If we have been ignorant or careless of Thy laws of health; if we have allowed our spirits to become a prey to worry, fear, or despair; if we have forgotten Thee, our Divine Physician, grant us Thy forgiveness, and help us to find in Thy loving power our health of body and our joy of soul. Through Jesus Christ our Lord. Amen.

—AUTHOR UNKNOWN

BEFORE AN OPERATION

God, our Father, whose love is stronger than the best human love, and whose care surrounds us every moment of life, prepare my body, mind, and spirit for the surgery planned to make me well. Cleanse my life of every unworthy deed and every accusing memory. Wash away every sin by Thy purifying and forgiving love. Help me to grow quiet, trustful, confident in the knowledge that Thou art here and wilt be with me when I am in the skilful hands of surgeons and nurses. Give every needed resource of skill and carefulness to him who will operate and to those who will assist. O Thou whose Son Jesus Christ is with me all the way, grant me quiet and refreshing rest as I hear Christ say, "*Let not your hearts be troubled, neither let them be afraid.*" For Thy love's sake. Amen.—DAVID A. MACLENNAN

> Good night, Lord;
> I'm very tired,
> But You were, too.
>
> Can't say much,
> But You know all;
> Even that I'm yawning.
>
> Good night, Lord,
> Secure my sleep;
> See You in the morning.[16]
> —CECIL HUNT

Jesus said: "*Come to me, all who labour and are heavy-laden, and I will give you rest. Take my yoke upon you, and learn from me; for I am gentle and lowly in heart, and you will find rest for your souls. For my yoke is easy, and my burden is light.*"—MATTHEW 11: 28-30

VII

The Healing Community

THE CHURCH—CHRIST AT WORK

Jesus Christ lives within and among His followers and friends today. He lives within His resurrection Body. His resurrection Body is the living Church, the people of God. This Church is the redemptive Community of the risen Lord. Of course when we speak of the Church in these terms, we mean something deeper, more inclusive, more divine than the buildings, denominations, or congregations which the living Church uses. To become visible in the world, the Body of Christ must employ organizations created and supported by fallible and often sinning human beings, even as you and I. It is true that the Church exists not primarily to heal the bodies and minds of distressed human beings, but to give God the glory through its worship of Him. This worship includes the preaching of "*the glorious gospel of the blessed God.*" This gospel is the story and the deed of God in the life, teaching, death, resurrection, and continued life of the Lord Jesus Christ.

In fulfilling the chief reason for its creation, the Church is the instrument of Christ's resurrection power. This power includes healing by God's Spirit, by the risen Lord. Christ is Saviour first, and then Healer. But He *is* Healer, and His Healing comes now often through His Body, the Church. Christians are Christ's hands, Christ's lips, Christ's heart. When Christ is given the pre-eminence by the Church, He proves Himself "*the same yesterday and today and for ever.*"

RELEASING HEALING POWER

How does the Church continue the healing ministry Christ exercised in

Palestine, as He went about doing good to all sorts of men, women, and children?

(1) *The Church demonstrates Christ's power as it reproduces the character of the apostolic Church.* Consider this description of the early Church in Acts 2: 42: "*They devoted themselves to the apostles' teaching and fellowship, to the breaking of bread and the prayers.*" Whenever a congregation of the Lord's people gives Christ the supreme place through teaching and preaching "*the truth as it is in Jesus*"; whenever a church devotes itself to demonstrating the all-inclusive love of Christ; whenever His lasting Supper is faithfully and joyfully observed and partaken (the Lord's Supper); whenever a church is a continuing company at prayer—there the power of the risen Lord is evident. "Where Christ is, there is the Church." The promise is positive that where the Lord Jesus is given a place in the Church through His Word, through His Supper, and through the Holy Spirit His presence is effectual.

Whenever an individual welcomes the

spirit of Christ into his life, he becomes a new person. Whenever a group of persons within the Church allows the risen life of Christ to direct their thinking and serving and praying, they become a new creation. "*If any man be in Christ, he is a new creature: . . . all things are become new*" (KJ.).

(2) *The Church acts in Christ's name and place when it encourages its members to confess their sins, accept His forgiveness, admit their failures, and take Christ's grace to begin again.* Today, as when the paralysed man was brought through the roof to Jesus for healing, our Lord seeks first to deal with our basic need, which often is for God's own pardon of what we have done. "*Confess your sins to one another,*" writes James, "*and pray for another, that you may be healed.*"

In recent years we have heard or read of what is called psychosomatic medicine. Psychosomatic means soul and body. Many, if not a majority, of our illnesses are psychosomatic. Experienced doctors have long known that many ailments are psychological or emotional in origin.

Repressing a sense of guilt, trying to "bury" inside us feelings of failure, fear, or hostility can upset our physical balance. Some medical research men believe that over seventy per cent of our illnesses are emotional in origin. Confession to the Church as the Church is represented by a pastor or other trusted Christian can bring healing when such acknowledgment of our failure is followed by prayer for God's forgiveness and our acceptance of His pardon.

(3) A third way in which Christ exercises His power through the Church to cure us of our diseases is *through the prayers of the Church*. The New Testament apostle who gave us the Epistle of James wrote:

Is any among you sick? Let him call for the elders of the church, and let them pray over him, anointing him with oil in the name of the Lord; and the prayer of faith will save the sick man, and the Lord will raise him up; and if he has committed sins, he will be forgiven. Therefore confess your sins to one another, and pray for one another, that you may be healed. The prayer of a righteous man has great power in its effects.

—JAMES 5: 14–16

"*The prayer of faith will save the sick man.*" This is true in the experience of countless numbers of pastors and lay people. Whether the symbolic use of oil to anoint the sick person is practised or not, the prayers of the Church do save the sufferer; and the Lord raises up the stricken soul. Intercessary prayer is not only the most unselfish prayer we can offer, it is the most effective, for it lifts those in need into the presence of the healing Christ. Such prayer, asking for specific help for particular individuals —naming them in His presence—mysteriously creates conditions in which the divine Physician can work His marvellous healing. Often prayer for one seriously ill places a kind of spiritual oxygen tent around the patient; new power to live seems to be given. True, baffling questions remain, such as: Why does one person so prayed for recover health and another person similarly prayed for does not?

Because the Church provides the ideal sanctuary in which Christ can make Himself known as Lord, as Saviour, and as Physician, be sure and ask for the Church's prayers. Do not be shy about asking the pastor or chaplain who visits you to remember you where it is best to be remembered—in the presence of the great and gracious God. Sometimes pastors hold services of healing. When such services are carefully planned, approved by the physician and the patient's family, and have as participants the minister, the patient, and close relatives or friends of the patient, these may be used of God to work healing. One of the twentieth-century's famous surgeons and biologists, the late Dr. Alexis Carrel, was convinced that the only condition indispensable to cure in many instances is prayer. "There is no need for the patient himself to pray," he wrote; "... it is sufficient that someone around him be in a state of prayer. Such facts are of profound significance.

... They prove the objective importance of the spiritual activities."

Therefore, to your own prayers add the prayers of others. Ask your family and friends to pray. Two or three gathered together in Christ's name make a better channel than separate people praying by themselves. If your home church has a prayer group, ask them to pray that your treatment may prove effective. Better still, ask them to pray that God's loving will for you and through you may be done. Jesus Christ can master anything which masters you. He works by direct action, and also frequently through His Church, which Dr. Wayne Oates rightly describes as "a healing community of concern."

PRAYERS

O God, who knowest the needs of all thy children, look with compassion upon thy sick (*Servant, child*) for whom our prayers are offered; give him [her] courage and confidence; bless those who minister to him [her] of thy healing

gifts and, if it be thy gracious will, restore him [her] to that perfect health which is thine alone to give; through Jesus Christ our Lord.[17]
— ROBERT N. RODENMAYER

Let us gather into the presence of Christ all who are suffering at this time all over the world, especially those who have no one to pray for them; and commend them to His love and care.

Lord Jesus, we bring in prayer to Thee every one at this time in weariness or pain upon the face of the earth. Far or near, with us or far from us, Lord, we beseech Thee for them—wherever they are, or whosoever they be. What help we would ask for ourselves from Thee, in their position, we pray Thee, O God of all comfort, to give it to them. Take them into Thy loving care and tend them. Be Thou very near to them, and supply all their need. This we ask of Thee, trusting in Thy love, who livest and reignest, world without end. Amen.[17]

Arranged by
— ARMEN D. JORJORIAN

A BLESSING

God our heavenly Father keep you always in His love, the Lord Jesus be your constant Companion, the Holy Spirit your never-failing Source of all sufficient grace to serve Him....[17]

Arranged by
—ARMEN D. JORJORIAN

THANKSGIVING FOR RECOVERY

O God, source of all health and goodness, we give thee humble and hearty thanks for the recovery of this thy (*child, servant*) from *his* sickness and for the return of strength. Bless all who have ministered to *him* of thy healing gifts, and send *him* on *his* way with a thankful heart and a cheerful spirit; through Jesus Christ our Lord.[17]

—ROBERT N. RODENMAYER

AUTHORS' INDEX

Bernanos, Georges, 52

Cairns, D. S., 39
Carrel, Alexis, 102
Cowie, Jan, 43-44

Dicks, Russell L., 74-75, 91

Hoch, Dorothee, 55
Hunt, Cecil, 95

Jones, E. Stanley, 54, 56
Jorjorian, Armen D., 104, 105

MacLennan, David A., 33-34, 94-95
Macleod, Fiona, 84
Maillard, John, 22
Mansfield, Katherine, 66-68
Miller, Samuel H., 60
Moffatt, James, 52, 54, 55
Moynihan, Lord, 9-10

Oates, Wayne, 103

Pennington, Chester A., 88-89
Phillips, J. B., 12, 48-49

Richard of Chichester, 46
Robison, Ruth, 58
Rodenmayer, Robert N., 103-104, 105

Sharpe, G. H., 93
Studdert-Kennedy, G. A., 72–73

Weatherhead, Leslie, D., 61–62, 79
Wood, Maurice, 59–60

Unknown authors and nine poets are not included in the index.

ACKNOWLEDGMENTS

[1] J. B. Phillips, *The New Testament in Modern English*, copyright 1958. Used by permission of The Macmillan Company. Geoffrey Bles, London.

[2] From "The Abbey Services of the Iona Community." Used by permission of the Iona Community, Glasgow, Scotland.

[3] From *Hospital Prayers*, 1944, the Committee on Public Worship and Aids to Devotion, The Church of Scotland. Used by permission.

[4] From *Daily Prayer*, edited by Eric Milner-White and G. W. Briggs, Oxford University Press, London. Used by permission.

[5] Used by permission of the Rev. Jan Cowie, Rosyth, Fife, Scotland.

[6] Georges Bernanos, *The Diary of a Country Priest*, copyright 1937. Used by permission of The Macmillan Company. Bodley Head, London.

[7] Dorothee Hoch, *Healing and Salvation*, Student Christian Movement Press Ltd., London. Used by permission.

[8] From *Everyman's Search* by Rebecca Beard. Arthur James Ltd., publishers of the United Kingdom and Commonwealth edition. Used by permission.

[9] Maurice Wood, *Your Suffering*, Hodder & Stoughton Ltd., London, publishers. Used by permission.

[10] Samuel H. Miller, *Prayers for Daily Use*. Hodder & Stoughton, London. Used by permission.

[11] Leslie D. Weatherhead, *The City Temple Tidings*, February 1958 issue. Used by permission.

[12] *The Journal of Katherine Mansfield*, published in 1927, Alfred A. Knopf, Inc. Used by permission. Constable, London.

[13] G. A. Studdert-Kennedy, *The Unutterable Beauty*, Hodder & Stoughton Ltd., London, publishers. Used by permission.

[14] Russell L. Dicks, *Toward Health and Wholeness*, Copyright 1960. Used by permission of The Macmillan Company, London.

[15] Used by permission of Dr. Chester A. Pennington.

[16] Cecil Hunt in *Uncommon Prayers*, arranged by John Wallace Suter. Published by Seabury Press in 1955. Used by permission.

[17] Prayers by Robert N. Rodenmayer and ones arranged by Armen D. Jorjorian are from *The Pastor's Prayerbook*, Robert N. Rodenmayer, editor. Oxford University Press, London & New York, 1960. Used by permission.